D0621103

DATE DUE

			Printed in USA

Venus

Earth

Neptune

The Life and Death of Stars

of Stars

The Life and Death of Stars

Ray Spangenburg and Kit Moser

Franklin Watts

A DIVISION OF SCHOLASTIC INC.
NEW YORK · TORONTO · LONDON · AUCKLAND
SYDNEY · MEXICO CITY · NEW DELHI · HONG KONG
DANBURY, CONNECTICUT

In memory of
CARL SAGAN,
*who brought the wonder
of the stars to all*

Photographs © 2003: Art Resource, NY: 42, 101 (Erich Lessing/Musee d'Art Moderne, Centre Pompidou, Paris, France), 16, 90 (H. Lewandowski); Aurora & Quanta Productions/ NASA/EAC Images: 57; Corbis Images: cover, 2, 60, 63, 74, 75, 78 (AFP), 35 (Lucien Aigner), 25 (Bettmann); NASA: 32, 97 (Don Figer), 72 (J.J. Hester/Arizona State University), 22, 23, 56, 58, 59, 77, 83, 102; Peter Arnold Inc.: 20 (Dennis Di Cicco), 17, 21 (Keller/ Schmidbauer/Astrofoto), 64 (NASA/Astrofoto), 29 (Yasumaro Yaita/Astrofoto); Photo Researchers, NY: 68 (Julian Baum/SPL), 37 (Adam Hart-Davis/SPL), 19, 93 (Laguna Design/SPL), 10 (NASA/SPL), 76 (Royal Observatory, Edinburgh/SPL), 52, 54, 66 (Space Telescope Science Institute/NASA/SPL); The Image Works: 12, 18, 89 (Photri/Topham), 24, 94; Woodfin Camp & Associates/Mireille Vautier: 14.

The photograph on the cover shows the development of a new star in the Milky Way Galaxy. The photograph opposite the title page shows a Hubble image of the giant nebula NGC 3603 illustrating the entire life cycle of stars.

Library of Congress Cataloging-in-Publication Data
    Spangenburg, Ray, 1939–
    The life and death of stars / Ray Spangenburg and Kit Moser.
    p. cm. — (Out of this world)
Summary: A comprehensive look at stars and their "life cycle," from humans' earliest observations of the constellations to recent discoveries about black holes and future space missions to study our Sun and other stars.
Includes bibliographical references and index.
    ISBN 0-531-11897-5 (lib. bdg.)   0-531-16685-6 (pbk.)
    1. Stars—Juvenile literature. [1. Stars.] I. Moser, Diane, 1944– II. Title.
III. Out of this world (Franklin Watts, Inc.)
QB801.7.S65 2003   523.8—dc21   2003005809

Acknowledgments

To all those who have contributed to *The Life and Death of Stars,* we would like to take this opportunity to say "thank you," with special appreciation to our editors on this project, Melissa Palestro and Christine Florie, for their enthusiasm and fine work. We would also like to give credit to Melissa Stewart, whose originality and vision provided the initial sparks for this series. Additionally, we would like to extend a great appreciation to Margaret Carruthers, planetary geologist, and Dr. Richard Ash of the University of Maryland, who both read the manuscript and provided—as in the past—many insightful and excellent suggestions. If any inaccuracies remain, the fault is ours, not theirs. Also, to Tony Reichhardt and John Rhea, once our editors at the former *Space World Magazine,* thanks for starting us out on the fascinating journey we have taken during our years of writing about space.

Contents

The Life and Death of Stars

By studying the life and death of stars, scientists hope to find clues to the greatest scientific mystery of all: the origin of life on Earth.

The Star Players

When you think about stars, you have to think big. About 95 percent of all visible matter in our Galaxy (the Milky Way)—and probably in the universe—is contained in stars. Most of the rest is interstellar gas and dust. Planets such as Earth are so small by comparison that, on this scale, they are insignificant. Most stars are huge. They are so enormous, we can hardly imagine their size. Our own Sun is just a medium-sized star and its diameter is more than 100 times greater than Earth's. Many stars are much, much bigger than the Sun. In fact, some exist that have diameters more that 1,000 times the Sun's. That's big.

These mammoth balls of glowing gas appear as mere tiny pinpricks of light to anyone standing on Earth looking up at the nighttime sky. Even with the largest telescopes, they still look tiny. That's

This *Hubble Space Telescope* image shows a jumble of young blue star clusters around the central region of the galaxy Centaurus A. Scientists believe that at the very center of the galaxy is a colossal black hole.

because all stars except for the Sun are enormously far away. The nearest is more than 25 trillion miles (40 trillion kilometers) from Earth. Its name is Proxima Centauri, also called Alpha Centauri C, and light from that star takes some *4.2 years* to travel the distance to Earth—at light's rapid rate of 186,000 miles (300,000 km) per second!

Most stars we see are also extremely old—usually about 10 billion years old, or more. New stars are constantly forming, though, in huge dust clouds within our *Galaxy* and in other galaxies (systems of stars, dust, and gas held together by gravity).

This book takes you on a voyage through the "life cycle" of stars—from birth through midlife to their later stages and death. Violent and powerful forces play parts in these cycles. Like giant nuclear fusion bombs, stars shine from the vast energy within them. They play out their stories, and they come to an end millions, or even billions of years later. Gravity plays an important role in their development and lives—and serves as a counterpoint to the evolution of the great expanding universe itself.

The ancient Maya civilization of Central America made remark-able astronomical observations. Seen here is the ruins of what is believed to have been an observatory at the Mayan city of Chichén Itzá, in the Yucatán peninsula of Mexico and Guatemala.

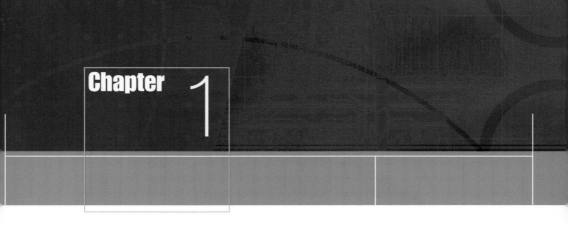

Chapter 1

Beginnings . . .

For as long as human beings have walked on Earth's surface, people have watched the stars. Ancient skywatchers observed the movement of the stars. As long as 10,000–11,000 years ago Mayan astronomers in Central America left behind inscriptions and constructions related to the movements of celestial objects. They observed the Milky Way and saw its crowds of stars as the "World Tree," the tree of life from which all life originated. In what is now Zaire, archaeologists have found an ancient bone with markings about 8,500–10,000 years old. They think it was probably used to mark the months and phases of the Moon. Egyptian skywatchers devised a calendar some 6,000–7,500 years ago. During the reign of the great Babylonian king Hammurabi, around 1750 B.C.E., astronomers compiled star catalogs

Humankind has always been fascinated by the stars. The ancient Babylonians carved star charts into stone.

and planetary records. Star watching, cataloging and record keeping have continued from at least that time on.

The Pawnee people of North America said the god Tirawa created the world and sent the stars to hold up the sky. Tirawa put the brightest stars to work managing the clouds, winds, and rain. These weather patterns governed the success of crops and the well-being of the Pawnee.

In Egypt, skywatchers noticed that when the star Sirius rose, it seemed to bring with it the yearly flooding of the Nile. Without this flooding, there would be no water for the crops and people would starve. So astronomers charted the time between the annual appearance of Sirius on the horizon.

The ancients saw patterns in the way some groups of stars were arranged. They gave names to these groups, or *constellations*, and they told stories about them. The Mayans saw the constellation we call the Pleiades and saw its resemblance to the tail of a rattlesnake. They called it "Tz'ab." The ancient Greeks told a story of seven sisters who were thrown into the sky to save them from a man who was chasing them. Ironically, the constellation Pleiades does contain seven stars, but the seventh is too dim to see without a telescope, which had not yet been invented—the ancient Greek astronomers didn't see it. To explain the presence of only six visible stars, they recounted that one of the seven

The constellation known as the Pleiades, seen here, has been known to humans since ancient times. They were mentioned by the Greek writer Hesiod in 1000 B.C.E., by Homer in the *Odyssey*, and three separate times in the Bible.

sisters ran away and hid because she was ashamed of her husband. That left the other six sisters to take their places as stars in the sky.

In Hindu mythology the same constellation has yet another story attached to it. The stars of the Big Dipper were seven sages, the Rishis. The sages were married to seven sisters, who were called Krittika. They lived together happily in the northern sky. However, the god of fire, named Agni, fell in love with the seven Krittika, the wives of the Rishis. Rejected, he wandered in loneliness until he met Svaha, the star we call Zeta Tauri (at the southern tip of the horns of the constellation Taurus). Svaha wanted to win Agni's heart, so she disguised herself as the seven Krittika. Rumors spread about Agni and the wives of the Rishis, and six of the seven were divorced by their husbands. The six wandered off in the skies to become the constellation that the Greeks called the Pleiades.

Every mythology had stories to explain and interpret the stars. Ancient skywatchers saw the stars march across the skies in regular cycles, and they usually saw the stars as agents of the gods or as gods themselves. These skywatchers saw and understood as accurately as they could, and their stories held a truth for their time. Today's view of the stars, though, is even more magnificent. Through technology and science, especially in the last 400 years, we have come to see the stars as part of the vast universe that to scientists' best current estimate began a little less than 14 billion years ago.

The Big Bang

Most astronomers or astrophysicists think that the universe began with a sudden, enormous, cataclysmic, and extremely rapid expansion from a single point. This event, known as the "Big Bang," was the beginning of all time and all space, known as space-time. All the building blocks of the universe were formed in the Big Bang—all the massive, far-flung matter that exists. (Sound does not travel in space because space is a *vacuum*. So there was no noise—no "big bang"—when the Big Bang occurred!)

At the beginning, or within a tiny fraction of a second after the beginning, the temperature was enormously hot—hotter than anyone can imagine—some billion trillion trillion degrees Celsius. The universe swelled with enormous speed and began rapidly cooling.

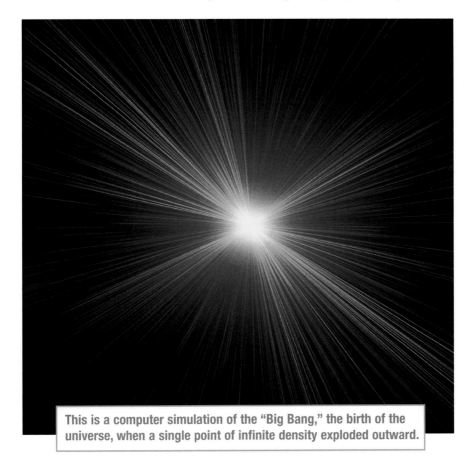

This is a computer simulation of the "Big Bang," the birth of the universe, when a single point of infinite density exploded outward.

Look upward into the nighttime sky at the billions of stars you can see. These are just a tiny part of the total universe. The stars we see are, for the most part, just the nearby, or "local" stars of our Galaxy, the Milky Way. About 200 billion to 300 billion stars exist in just this galaxy alone. Most galaxies are found in clusters with other galaxies— sometimes as many as a thousand of them. Our Galaxy belongs to a cluster of about three dozen galaxies known as the Local Group.

Distances in space are vast. Remember, Proxima Centauri (part of the Alpha Centauri star system), the nearest star aside from our Sun, is 4.2 light years away. That is, the light we see tonight shows what Prox-

In this photo, the Milky Way appears as the filmy strip running vertically above the horizon. The Milky Way is the galaxy that contains our solar system.

ima Centauri looked like 4.2 years ago. The Milky Way is so huge that light takes 80,000 years to cross from one side to the other—still traveling at 186,000 miles (300,000 km) per second.

The Local Group is only a small part of the universe. The great mountaintop observatories and the mirrors, cameras, and other instruments of the *Hubble Space Telescope* (*HST*), the *Chandra X-ray Telescope*, and others let us look beyond our own Galaxy, into deep space. There, we catch sight of other huge galaxies of stars. The Andromeda Galaxy, known to scientists as M31, is the closest galaxy, and it is about 2 million light years away. Some very old galaxies are billions of light

This is the spiral galaxy M31, known also as Andromeda. Easily visible to the naked eye, Andromeda received its first mention by a Persian astronomer in 964. Today, it is the most widely studied galaxy other than our own.

Today's sophisticated deep-space imaging instruments allow scientists to view space objects in other than visible light. This is a mosaic of X-ray images of the Milky Way captured by NASA's *Chandra X-ray Telescope.*

years away. M31 is the most distant object visible to the human eye without a telescope (although, without a telescope you can't tell what it's made of—it just looks like a fuzzy patch in the sky).

Like many galaxies, Andromeda has spiral arms extending outward from a bulging center, but galaxies come in all shapes and sizes. The

Milky Way also has spiral arms, and our solar system lies on the inner edge of one of those arms. The spiral arms contain quantities of dust and interstellar gas held together by gravity. There, new stars are often born.

There are billions of galaxies in the universe. However, before 1924, less than 100 years ago, scientists weren't sure whether or not the

This is a spiral galaxy, NGC 4622, in the constellation Centaurus. It is of special interest to astronomers because one of its "arms" seems to spiral in a different direction than the other two.

Milky Way was the only galaxy. American astronomer Edwin P. Hubble (1889–1953)—after whom the space telescope *HST* was named— was the first to show that many stars were too distant to be part of our own Galaxy. Thanks to Hubble, we now know that the fuzzy

"Andromeda Nebula" (so named because it looked like a cloud) is really a galaxy. Hubble came up with distances for nine other galaxies. Scientists now know that many billions of galaxies exist, and each galaxy contains many billions of stars.

After the Big Bang, an expansion began that has never stopped. (If it did, the force of gravity would take over and we would all be crushed by inward-falling mass.) All these galaxies—all objects and systems in the universe, in fact—are moving *away* from our Galaxy and from each other, at steadily increasing speeds.

Working with a talented astronomer named Milton Humason, Edwin Hubble also was first to observe that every galaxy or galaxy cluster was moving away from every other—and that the universe was

expanding. He also saw that the galaxies were moving at a rate proportional to their distance, so that the farther away they were, the faster they were moving. This insight became known as "Hubble's Constant." It is fitting that in 1999 *HST*, the space telescope named after Hubble, provided the first precise measurements of these movements—an essential ingredient for telling the age, size, and future of the universe.

Edwin Hubble takes a look through the Schmidt telescope at the Palomar Observatory in California. Hubble used the change in the spectrum of visible light from stars to determine that the universe is expanding.

From Mules to Photographic Plates

American astronomer Milton Humason (1891–1972) knew how to ask questions, had a wonderful knack for using a telescope to photograph the skies, and soaked up books on astronomy. In those ways he may not have been very different from other astronomers, but the path he took to his career was unique. Humason left school after the eighth grade, and he began working as a mule packer, hauling supplies up the steep mountainside trail to the Mount Wilson Observatory, north of Los Angeles. Later, he got jobs busing dishes in the cafeteria there and sweeping out the observatory. These positions gave him glimpses of an astronomer's work, and he knew that was what he wanted to do. That's when he started really studying and reading and talking to the astronomers at the observatory.

His first big opportunity came when he was offered a position assisting with one of the smaller telescopes. In his spare time, he studied, read, and learned as much as he could about the stars, telescopes, and ways of finding out about the universe. He continued to take on other projects, and by 1928, he had become Edwin Hubble's close collaborator.

Working with Hubble, Humason began carefully measuring the light of thousands of remote galaxies. He was a keen and dedicated observer, and he became expert at gathering data from faint, distant galaxies. He measured both the velocity of these galaxies and their distance. Humason's observations served to verify Hubble's law, which states that all galaxies in the universe are moving farther and farther apart and that the most distant galaxies are retreating fastest. Humason's work helped establish what is still found to be the case today—that Hubble's law holds true throughout the observable universe.

Scientists have since figured out—judging by how fast the most distant galaxies are moving away from us—that the expansion of the universe began a little less than 14 billion years ago. No one knows where all the material came from, but scientists think that before the Big Bang, there was nothing. All of the energy in the universe was created in the Big Bang, much of which converted to mass in that single event that began everything. (Mass and energy readily convert back and forth.)

That is how the first stars began some 14 billion years ago. Ever since then, stars have continued to be "born." Many shine brightly for billions of years. Then, finally, they "die." Before plunging into the life story of stars, though, let's take a look at a few facts about stars—what they are and what they are like.

Starry Diversity

Standing on a hilltop on a summer night looking up at the sky, if the night is clear and not too many urban lights spoil the view, you can see clusters and sprinklings of tiny bright lights. From this vantage point, who would ever imagine the immense size of some of these intensely bright objects, the immense heat, the varied distances, and the many different guises they come in. Like people, stars have a life cycle—they spend millions or billions of formative years as infant stars before reaching a steady, stable state. Some stars never do. Some blow up in giant explosions. There are small stars and medium-sized stars, large stars, and enormous stars. There are large, luminous blue giants, and small, dim, red ones. Others come in yellow, like our Sun, or bright orange like some supergiants. We know some have planets, and some travel with a companion star, forming two-star systems. Some stars wink or pulse or collapse.

T Tauri Stars

T Tauri stars are young stars—just emerging from the protostar, or infant pre-star stage, blowing off the dust and gas of the "star nursery." They are often similar to our Sun, often seen in molecular clouds— very cold, large clouds of complex organic molecules found in our

Galaxy. They are usually brighter than our Sun and rotate much faster—making a full rotation in a few days, a trip that takes the Sun a month.

Binaries: Stars That Are "Hitched"

You've probably heard the expression, "Hitch your wagon to a star." Well, in some cases, two stars are, in a way, hitched to each other. A pair of binary stars, also known as a binary star system, are attracted to each other gravitationally. They move in orbit around a common point called the center of mass. In some cases, more than two stars are involved, and then they are called "multiples." Binary or multiple stars may be so close together that discerning separate bodies is difficult. Scientists estimate that as many as two-thirds of all stars belong to binary or multiple star systems. Alpha Centauri, the star system that is closest to the Sun, is a multiple star system. Binary or multiple stars can come in several flavors.

- *Visual binaries* form a binary system that is visibly composed of separate bodies when viewed through a telescope. In 1803, English astronomer William Herschel (1738–1822) pointed out the resemblance of the orbits in these star systems to the relationship between Earth and the Moon.

- In an *eclipsing binary*, the stars in the system vary in brightness. This variation was first explained by English astronomer John Goodricke in 1782. He suspected that when one of the two stars eclipsed the other, blocking out its light, the brightness took a dip, and he was right.

Sirius is the brightest star in the night sky and is twice as massive as the Sun. Sirius is an example of a binary star system. Its companion star, Sirius B, was the first white dwarf star discovered.

- A *spectroscopic binary* has elements that orbit so close together that astronomers can only tell the system is a binary from its spectrum.

- In X-ray binaries, one component is very compact—probably in the last stages of its life. It may be a *white dwarf* such as Sirius. It may be a *neutron star*. It may even be a *black hole*. They are called X-ray binaries because they give off X-ray radiation, detectable with an X-ray telescope. The X-ray radiation may vary in intensity, if the two bodies of the binary periodically eclipse each other.

Sometimes binaries are so close together that they trade mass back and forth, and they are known as semidetached binaries. Some astronomers think that these binaries may even sometimes join together, or coalesce.

Pulsating Variable Stars

These stars change in brightness over time either predictably in a pattern, or randomly.

Flare Stars

Some red dwarf stars produce flares the way our own Sun does—but these flares are huge, visibly increasing the star's brightness from several light years away. Proxima Centauri, the closest star to the solar system aside from the Sun, is a flare star.

Neutron Stars

At the opposite end of the star lifetime from the T Tauri star, a neutron star has run out of fuel and collapsed, causing all its atomic particles to pack tightly together in a tight cluster of neutrons.

Pulsars

These neutron stars are not only densely packed collapsed stars, but they also send out a pulsing stream of radio signals.

Black Holes

Among the most mysterious stellar objects, black holes are also dense star remnants—but these objects have become so dense that nothing, not even light, can escape the region surrounding them known as the "event horizon." Anything that enters that region will never leave.

Near the center of our galaxy lies The Quintuplet Star Cluster.
It was formed approximately four million years ago.

Chapter 2

What Is a Star?

Today we know that stars are not pillars that hold up the canopy of the heavens or pinpricks in a planetarium sky. Scientists now know that stars are the main source of all the light we see, day and night. Even the light of the Moon is the reflected light of the Sun—our own star. Like the Moon, the planets generally give off no light of their own—they, too, reflect the light of the Sun. Most of the other points of light we see in the nighttime skies are stars, or groups of stars. They shine with a powerful luminosity that spans vast distances—even billions of light years. The enormous light of these huge, fascinating objects comes from deep within.

What makes stars shine so brightly?

Power from the Core

The heartbeat of every star begins at its core. There, nuclear reactions are the source of the massive energy it produces. These reactions are called "nuclear" reactions because they take place inside atoms—within their nuclei (plural of nucleus). The nuclear reactions at the star's center drive all the other reactions that take place in the star's many layers of gas, including power violent eruptions at the surface. This immense release of energy that travels from the core to the surface is what makes stars so bright.

This fact has not always been obvious, though. In the 1860s, two physicists, William Thomson (Baron Kelvin of Largs) and Hermann von Helmholtz, first explored some key questions about what went on deep inside the Sun, our own local star—and the easiest one to study. These scientists realized that the force of gravity holding the Sun's mass together must create an immense squeeze within the Sun. The pressure of the Sun's mass pushing inward must generate enormous heat—as high as 40 million°F (22 million°C). When an object is hotter than the surrounding material, the heat radiates away from the object. When this happens, the object cools and shrinks, or contracts—pressing inward even more—and this pressure produces more heat. Expansion and contraction continues, over and over. Thomson and Helmholtz thought they had discovered what powered the Sun—and all the stars.

For the Sun, physicists calculated that this source of energy would last a very long time—100 million years. So initially they concluded that the conversion of gravitational energy into heat seemed like a good explanation for the Sun's radiance, or "starshine." However, as scientists soon began to discover, 100 million years was not long enough! Earth, the Sun, and the planets had actually been around a lot longer than that already—4.5 billion years, as we know now.

A better explanation didn't come along right away, though. It had to wait for physicists to begin discovering the structure of the atom. It had to wait for Albert Einstein's theory of relativity. It had to wait for quantum mechanics, the theory that all particles have wave properties. Before anyone could come up with a better explanation, scientists would have to recognize that the composition of the Sun and the stars was mainly hydrogen. All these discoveries began to build on each other in rapid succession at the beginning of the twentieth century.

In 1926, Sir Arthur Eddington (1882–1944) put the first piece of the puzzle in place. He based his work on Einstein's famous equation $e = mc^2$. (In this equation, e stands for energy, m stands for mass, and c stands for a constant, the speed of light, which is always the same in a vacuum.) Since light travels at tremendous speed, 186,000 miles (300,000 km) per second, this equation shows that a very small amount of mass is required to create enormous energy.

Eddington looked at the atomic weights of hydrogen and helium. From this evidence, he figured out that four hydrogen atoms could combine in a process called atomic fusion (nuclear

Albert Einstein relaxes in his study at Princeton, New Jersey. Einstein's theory about space and time revolutionized our understanding of the universe.

fusion) to form one helium atom, with a loss of atomic weight of 0.7 percent. He was exploring a hunch. If his hunch were right, then that weight loss could account for an enormous release of energy. Eddington thought: Suppose that the mass of the Sun were pure hydrogen. Then it could produce energy in this way for 10 billion years. Now the time span fit what geologists already knew about the age of Earth and the solar system.

However, Eddington had not yet quite proved his point. Did the Sun have enough hydrogen to fuel this process for as long as he had estimated? Physicist Cecilia Payne-Gaposchkin (1900-1979) cleared up this part of the problem. She showed that hydrogen is the main ingredient of all stars.

Nuclear Fusion at Work

Hydrogen is the most common element in the universe, and now that we know that, it may not be so surprising to us that the stars contain a lot of it. What may be more surprising is that there's comparatively little hydrogen on Earth.

It all has to do with pull. Hydrogen is the lightest of all the elements, so it easily escapes from bodies in the solar system that do not have a lot of mass (and, therefore, not a lot of gravity). Huge, massive bodies, though, have enough gravitational pull to keep hydrogen from escaping. Stars are huge. Our Sun has a mass so great that if you rolled up all the planets in the solar system into a single ball, you would have to put together 1,000 such balls to equal the Sun's mass.

A star has attracted such enormous quantities of hydrogen that as the layers of gas are pulled by the star's gravity, they press in crushingly

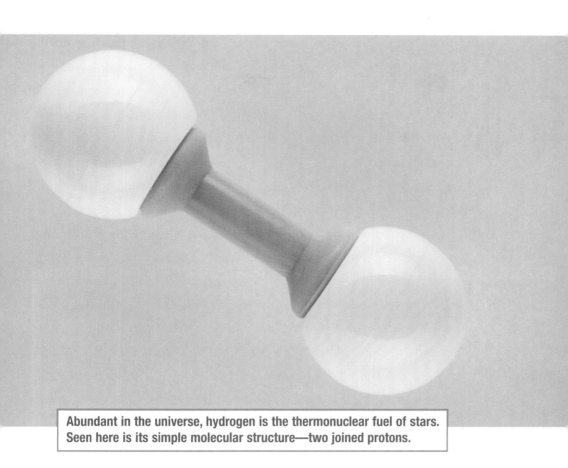

Abundant in the universe, hydrogen is the thermonuclear fuel of stars. Seen here is its simple molecular structure—two joined protons.

on the center, or core. There, extreme heat and pressure cause hydrogen to fuse into helium, which is four times as heavy (though still not a heavy gas). This reaction produces the energy of the stars.

Nuclear fusion in a star is the same nuclear fusion process that takes place during the explosion of a hydrogen bomb. The energy released when hydrogen becomes helium is identical. However, far more hydrogen fuel is available in a star than in a bomb, and the release of energy is enormously more powerful.

As the process begins in the star's interior, hydrogen is stripped of its single electron by extreme pressure and heat. This process results in releasing the single unbound proton of the hydrogen nucleus and changes hydrogen gas into a *plasma*, a state of matter made up of unbound negative electrons and positive ions, which may conduct electrical current.

This single proton, moving randomly among other protons jumbled together in the core, goes through a tediously long process of banging into other protons and repelling them, and then colliding again, over and over. Because all these particles have the same positive charge, they don't naturally attract each other, so they keep on moving. With each collision some protons gain a little energy and others lose energy. Some protons with the highest energy (the hottest protons) can overcome the repulsion caused by the charge of another proton and two fuse together. This liberates some energy and produces a deuterium nucleus (a hydrogen nucleus consisting of a neutron and a proton). This combination is very unstable, though, and soon reacts with another proton to form helium-3, a nucleus with two protons and a neutron (instead of helium's normal one proton and one neutron). The helium-3 nucleus then reacts with another helium-3 nucleus to produce two protons and a helium-4 nucleus (also called an alpha particle), composed of helium's usual 2-proton nucleus and an additional two neutrons—a very stable structure. In the process, the two extra protons from the two helium-3 nuclei are ejected, along with the release of considerable energy and some tiny particles called *neutrinos*. Each of these steps produces energy.

The initial high temperature in the core of the Sun comes from contraction (potential energy transformed into kinetic energy), but after that it becomes self-sustaining, with the additional energy coming from fusion. This prevents further contraction (until the hydrogen starts to run low—then there will be contraction and the temperature will rise again and a whole new set of reactions will start that consume helium, while the hydrogen reactions also continue).

The distribution of energy between hydrogen atoms during the lifetime of the star is determined by the temperature of the star. The mean speed of the atom gives the temperature, but there is a distribution of speeds around this mean speed (energy)—some collide with other hydrogen nuclei, but the distribution of energy stays the same. An individual hydrogen atom does not have a fixed energy throughout the life of the star-—sometimes it is low, sometimes high—but it is always in a state of flux. Then, finally, fusion with another proton can take place.

If this process is so hit-and-miss and takes so long, how can this nuclear powerhouse work? How does it keep going? It works because the Sun's core has an enormous number of these protons. While one proton is still 10 billion years away from fusion, many others are on their threshold at any given moment.

The beauty of this process is that it is stable and long-term. This explains why humans have long held the opinion that the Sun is a reliable, predictable source of energy.

Classifying Stars

When you look up at the nighttime skies, you see some stars that seem very bright. Others are dim and faint. Yet many of the faint stars are really much more luminous than those that seem so bright. They seem dim because they are enormously far away.

The challenge to astronomers is how to find out about stars across the vast distances of space. What is their true nature and how can you classify them and sort them into groups that make sense?

How Bright?

At least 2,000 years ago astronomers began to work out a system for sorting the stars by brightness. The Greek astronomer Hipparchus set up a system for sorting stars into six different levels of brightness, called magnitudes. The first magnitude included the most luminous stars. The sixth magnitude was reserved for the faintest stars that people could see. The bright star Sirius is first magnitude. Polaris (the North Star) is second magnitude and so are most of the stars in the Big Dipper. The stars in the handle of the Little Dipper are fourth magnitude. It takes a dark, clear night away from city or suburban lights to see a fifth magnitude (such as the faintest star in the Little Dipper's bowl), or a sixth magnitude star.

This early system of sorting stars is still used by astronomers—but it really measures visually apparent magnitude. That is, how luminous a star appears to be. That may be far different from a star's true luminosity when an adjustment is made for its distance from Earth.

Star Motions

Astronomers from the sixteenth century on knew that Earth orbited the Sun (established by Nicolaus Copernicus and published by him in 1543). They knew that the stars therefore showed an annual change, called a *parallax*, that caused them to seem to shift.

Stars also show changes in right ascension (the "longitude" of the sky) and declination (the "latitude" of the sky). That is, they change position in the skies. This discovery was made in 1718 by the English astronomer Edmond Halley. *Proper motions* (movements perpendicular to the viewer's line of sight) have been recorded for some tens of thousands of stars. These changes are small each year, but over centuries they have made visible changes in the patterns we call constellations.

Sorting by Color, Temperature, and Spectra

The star Betelgeuse, as most amateur astronomers know, is red. The star Sirius is white, and our Sun is yellow. What do these differences in color mean? They are indicators of different temperatures of the stars. Red stars are the coolest (though still a very hot 3,000 K). Yellow stars, such as the Sun and a star called Capella, have surface temperatures around 6,000 K. White stars rise to about 10,000 K, and blue stars are the hottest—some 20,000 degrees K or more.

The light we see is part of an important family of energies known as the *electromagnetic spectrum* (the full range of the waves and frequencies of electromagnetic radiation). Visible light is just about in the middle of the spectrum—the portion of the spectrum that we describe as the different colors of the rainbow, from red to violet. Red is made up of longer *wavelengths* of light, while violet is made up of shorter wavelengths. (A wavelength, or frequency, is the distance between wave crests on a wave of light or other radiation.) White light (sunlight and starlight) is a mixture of many of these colors. The rest of the electromagnetic spectrum is made up of types of radiation that humans cannot see, including radio waves, radar, infrared (all having relatively long wavelengths or frequencies) and ultraviolet radiation, X rays, and gamma rays (all having relatively short wavelengths).

Everything has its own characteristic spectrum. That is, every object absorbs some wavelengths of light and reflects others. For exam-

The Russian artist Wassily Kandinsky (1866–1944), whose *Red Spot* is seen here, is considered a master of color. An artist uses color in a painting to impart information and to affect the observer's response. Likewise, scientists can use the colors in various images of the stars to derive information about such things as their distance, their brightness, and their age.

ple, grass (or really, the chlorophyll in grass) reflects a lot of wavelengths in the green part of the spectrum. Goldfish reflect a lot in the yellow and orange part of the spectrum. When we look at things and observe their color, we use a natural form of spectroscopy to identify them by their color. Objects that generate energy, such as the Sun and other stars, also emit a characteristic spectrum.

Isaac Newton (1642–1727) was the first scientist to examine the spectrum of light in detail. He used a prism to split sunlight into different colors. More than a century later, in 1814, a German optician named Joseph von Fraunhofer (1787–1826) was working with the light that comes from the Sun. He noticed that sunlight created a spectrum that was marked by a number of dark lines. These lines in a spectrum are still known as "Fraunhofer lines." However, Fraunhofer could not figure out what the lines meant.

That mystery was solved by Gustav Kirchhoff (1824–1887), a German physicist. In 1859 he discovered that atoms in the upper layers of the Sun absorb some of the light before it leaves the Sun and travels to Earth, where he was observing. The upper layers of the Sun, or any star, are cooler than the lower regions. As light is generated by the heat below and travels to the surface, it is absorbed as it passes through the cooler gases above. The dark lines in the spectrum indicate that light has been absorbed in particular regions of the spectrum, leaving an absence of light, or darkness. Without a spectroscope or a prism, you would never notice the absence of these particular wavelengths. They are absent because a specific element (atom or ion) or molecule (rare in stars) has absorbed particular wavelengths of light. Each element blocks particular wavelengths of the spectrum—so each element leaves its own signature, a unique set of blocked wavelengths or, put another way, a unique pattern of dark lines. Because each different chemical makes a different pattern of lines—almost like a fingerprint—Kirchhoff realized that it is possible to recognize the chemical makeup of any star (including the Sun) by observing the spectrum its light produces.

But what if there were nothing to block the light? You would have a spectrum with no dark lines. That spectrum would be the star's background spectrum, which indicates the star's temperature. The hotter the star, the higher its energy output, and the higher the frequencies and the shorter the wavelengths it emits. Each star emits an entire range of frequencies, but its peak emission—where most of the light is emitted—indicates temperature. The background spectrum for an extremely hot star is at the blue end of the spectrum, while a cooler star will show peak emissions clustered at the red end of the spectrum. The coolest stars of all—the white dwarfs—show a background spectrum at even higher frequencies (longer wavelengths). The absorption lines indicating elements are superimposed on these background spectra (plural of spectrum).

Scientists can also gain information about a star's movement from its spectrum. This principle was first discovered in 1842 by Christian Johann Doppler (1803–1853), who found that a shift in a star's spectrum toward the red end indicates movement away from the observer, and movement toward the blue end indicates the object is approaching. This handy tool, known as the Doppler effect, has played a major part in observing and understanding the movement of stars and the expansion of the universe. A familiar example of this effect—in sound waves instead of light waves—is the rising (higher frequency) pitch of an approaching ambulance siren and its falling (lower frequency) pitch as it speeds away.

Kirchoff worked with German chemist Robert Bunsen (1811–1899) to invent an instrument, the spectroscope, for observing and identifying the spectra of all the elements known at the time. They even discovered a few no one knew about yet. In 1868 French astronomer Pierre Janssen observed strange spectra while viewing a solar eclipse in India. He sent the data to English astronomer Joseph Lockyer, who realized the spectra represented a new element, helium—one that had not yet ever been observed on Earth. This discovery proved key to understanding the workings of the Sun. Examination of the Sun's atmosphere using spectroscopy provided a powerful method for identifying the signatures, or fingerprints, of stars.

Spectroscopes can identify the wavelengths of starlight precisely, as well as the portions of the electromagnetic spectrum that humans can't see, such as infrared, ultraviolet, and radio waves.

The American astronomer Edward C. Pickering (1846–1919) began the task of assigning classifications to stars based on their spectra. He assigned letters of the alphabet based on the strength of a star's hydrogen line in its spectrum. The strongest received an A, B came next, and so on, as far as the letter O. The classifications roughly matched the color of the stars as well, from white to yellow to red. Only O was out of order, since O stars were blue-white and really belonged before A. Once his researchers began using the system, they saw the need for a few other adjustments. The letters C, D, and E turned out to be unnecessary, so they ended up using the sequence OBAFGKM.

One of his researchers, Annie Jump Cannon, discovered that the original system was a little too crude, once observations improved. So she added numbers to the letters, assigning 0 through 9 to each letter classification. Our Sun has a classification of G2.

Understanding Types of Stars

Around the turn of the twentieth century, a Danish amateur astronomer and popularizer named Ejnar Hertzsprung (1873–1967) began looking for a way to deal with the fact that a dim star close at hand can appear brighter than a faraway star that is actually much brighter. How can you show how bright stars really are? Astronomers had a way to measure luminosity, but in reality these measurements were useful primarily for finding a star in the sky. This measurement had little to do with the real nature of the star, and he wanted to find a way to compare stars as they really were.

Hertzsprung invented a system for comparing the brightness of stars by imagining them all at the same distance from the observer—the absolute magnitude. He chose the distance of 10 parsecs—32 light years, or a little over 190 trillion miles (about 300 trillion km). (A parsec is the distance at which a star has a parallax of one second—see "Measuring Distances in the Universe" on page 50.) As early as 1905, Hertzsprung worked on the relationship of the color of stars and their absolute luminosity. However, he published his work in popular magazines, and he was an amateur astronomer, so professional astronomers unfortunately didn't pay much attention at first.

Star Classifier: Annie Jump Cannon

Annie Jump Cannon (1863–1941) graduated from Wellesley College in Massachusetts when she was 20. Astronomy fascinated her, and she returned to both Wellesley and Radcliffe College ten years later to continue her studies in astronomy. In 1896 she began work on a project led by Edward C. Pickering, director of the Harvard Observatory. Pickering called the many women he hired his "computers"— years before the electronic computer and the "PC" were invented. Cannon became one of them and she became the most famous.

Pickering had come up with a breakthrough idea for studying the spectra of stars ("stellar spectra"). Up to then, photographs of stellar spectra were taken one at a time by placing a prism between the starlight and a photographic plate (used instead of film). Pickering realized that if you put a large prism in front of a large photographic plate, the result would be a photograph of the spectra for all the stars on the plate. Each star appeared in the photograph as a tiny spectrum instead of a point of light. This made collecting the data much more efficient.

Cannon developed a system for classifying these photographs of stellar spectra. Her system remained in use for many years. She also found that the spectra could be arranged into a continuous series, so one could identify the stars on the basis of temperature, from hottest to coolest. Her work became the basis for the Henry Draper Catalogue, which grew to include classifications of 225,300 stars brighter than the ninth or tenth magnitude. Most of these were done single-handedly by Cannon herself.

Cannon once wrote: "Classifying the stars has helped materially in all studies of the structure of the Universe. No greater problem is presented to the human mind." In 1921, at a time when few women earned doctorates, Cannon became the first woman to receive a doctor of astronomy degree from Groningen University in the Netherlands. In 1925 Oxford University in England awarded Cannon an honorary doctorate. She earned many other prizes and awards for her work, but perhaps the most treasured was the award of the Draper Medal from the National Academy of Sciences in 1931. Astronomer Harlow Shapley, who presented the award, called the Draper Medal "one of the highest honors attainable by astronomers of any sex, race, religion, or political preference."

Cannon worked long, tedious hours on her research and made an enormous contribution to her field, but her data analysis and stellar classification were not her only gifts. Among her other talents, according to Shapley, Cannon was "author of nine immortal volumes, and several thousand oatmeal cookies," and she danced the Virginia reel and played bridge avidly.

Nearest Stars to Earth[1]

Vital Statistics

Name of Star	Distance from Earth in Light Years	Apparent Magnitude[2]	Absolute Magnitude
SUN	—	-26.8	4.75
PROXIMA CENTAURI (ALPHA CENTAURI C)	4.2	11.05 (var.)	15.5
RIGIL KENTAURUS (ALPHA CENTAURI A)	4.3	-0.1	4.3
ALPHA CENTAURI B	4.3	1.5	5.8
BARNARD'S STAR	5.9	9.5	13.2
WOLF 359	7.6	13.5 (var.)	16.8
LALANDE 21185	8.1	7.5	10.4
LUYTEN 726-8A UV	8.9	12.5 (var.)	15.3
LUYTEN 726-8B UV	8.9	13.0 (var.)	15.8
SIRIUS A (ALPHA CANIS MAJOR A)	8.6	-1.5	1.4
SIRIUS B (ALPHA CANIS MAJOR B)	8.6	7.2	11.5
ROSS 154	9.4	10.6	13.3
ROSS 248	10.3	12.2	14.8
EPSILON ERIDANI	10.7	3.7	6.13
LUYTEN 789-6	10.8	12.2	14.6

Name of Star	Distance from Earth in Light Years	Apparent Magnitude[2]	Absolute Magnitude
Ross 128	10.8	11.1	13.5
61 Cygnus A	11.2	5.2 (var.)	7.6
61 Cygnus B	11.2	6.0	8.4
Epsilon Ind	11.2	4.7	7.0
Procyon A (Alpha Canis Minor A)	11.4	0.4	2.7
Procyon B (Alpha Canis Minor B)	11.4	10.8	13.1

[1] Based on Bill Baity, Center for Astrophysics and Space Sciences (CASS), University of California at San Diego: http://casswww.ucsd.edu/public/nearest.html

[2] The lower the number, the brighter the magnitude, so the brightest apparent magnitudes are the largest negative numbers. In the column showing absolute magnitude, the lower numbers indicate greater magnitude.

Apparent magnitude may also be variable, especially in the case of stars such as Proxima Centauri, which is occasionally eclipsed by its larger companions.

At the same time, without knowing about Hertzsprung's work, an American astronomer named Henry Norris Russell (1877–1957) came up with some of the same ideas. The work of the two men is represented by a diagram called the Hertzsprung-Russell diagram of star luminosity. Since that is such a mouthful, most people just call it the H-R diagram for short.

The H-R diagram arranges information known about star forms to make them easier to study by providing a visual way to organize and track their relationships. It reflects the efforts made by the two

Measuring Distances in the Universe

A parallax is an important concept in astronomy—one that astronomers have been using since the time of the ancient Greeks and earlier. A parallax is the distance a star appears to change position when viewed against the same background from two different positions on Earth.

The two observation positions on Earth and the actual position of the star form a triangle. If you know the angles at each observation point, you can use geometry to figure out the angle (parallax) formed at the object by the two lines of sight when they meet. (The angles in a triangle always add up to 180 degrees.) Using some basic trigonometry, you can also figure out the distance to the star if you know the parallax and the distance between the two observation points (the baseline).

astronomers to bring order out of the chaos of data based on their studies of the relationships between the absolute magnitudes of stars and their spectral types or surface temperatures (or colors). The vertical axis of the diagram shows absolute magnitude (absolute luminosity) and the horizontal axis shows spectral class.

Once the position of a large number of stars is plotted on the diagram, it becomes easy to see that by far most stars fall in a broad band that extends from the bottom right (the dimmest and the coolest) to the top left (the brightest and the hottest). These are the "main sequence" stars—the dwarfs. Our Sun is a G2 dwarf. Dwarfs are not necessarily really small. The Sun has about average mass and is, overall, an average, ordinary star. About 90 percent of all stars you can see in the sky are main-sequence stars. They include stars of all colors and their magnitude varies widely. They have medium-sized diameters—the smallest diameters are about a tenth the diameter of the Sun's, and the largest are about ten times the Sun's.

Another band extends from the bottom left of the diagram to the top right (bright, yet cool). That is, brightness is increasing as the temperature drops. Russell called this group the giants, and they are huge. Compared with these stars, main-sequence stars are truly dwarfs. The giants also hold clues about the course of stellar evolution—the life and death of stars.

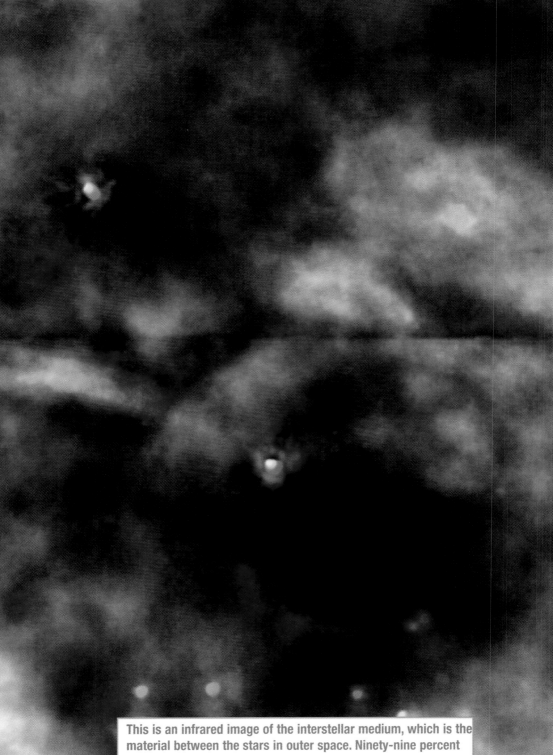

This is an infrared image of the interstellar medium, which is the material between the stars in outer space. Ninety-nine percent of the interstellar medium is gas, either hydrogen or helium.

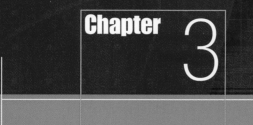

Chapter 3

Star Nurseries and Young Stars

The regions between stars and galaxies are not empty—far from it. These vast areas, sometimes called the "interstellar medium," are a mixture of dust and gas. The mixture is lumpy, has very, very low density, and is widely scattered. It is so low density that most people would consider it to be a vacuum. Yet these clouds of sparse dust can block out light from faraway stars. In our own Milky Way, they are visible as dark regions among the stars.

In the eighteenth century a philosopher and physicist from Prussia (now Germany) named Immanuel Kant (1724–1804) came up with the idea that stars like the Sun formed from a cloud, or nebula. He believed that stars took shape out of a stellar nebula formed from the smattering of dust and gas that is widely scattered throughout the universe. Kant thought that this thin veil of material would be unstable. Eventually, it would clump together into large clouds. These clouds would naturally rotate, shrinking and collapsing inward as they spun. The rotation would spin the nebula out into a flattened disk. Our solar system, Kant reasoned, grew out of such a process.

In the 1960s, astronomers began using radio telescopes to see through the dark, dusty clouds where stars are forming. In the 1990s the *Hubble Space Telescope* began taking images of star nurseries. At the

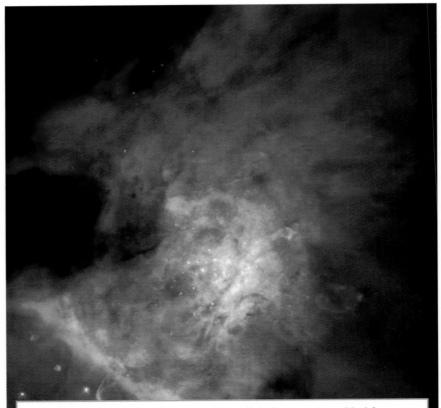

This panorama of the center of the Orion Nebula was assembled from many different individual images. It shows the nebula, in NASA's words, as a "churning, turbulent star factory" amid "flowing, luminescent gas."

heart of the Orion Nebula, it has captured views of a complex of *molecular clouds* that gives off great quantities of *ultraviolet (UV)* light. This area of the universe shows up beautifully in images taken in the UV region of the electromagnetic spectrum. There, in the center of the Orion Nebula, a great many stars are in the early stages of formation. This giant stellar nursery is about 1,600 light years away, and these stars are very young, for stars—only a few million years old.

Birth of a Star

Scientists have not figured out exactly what happens in a stellar nursery. They think it must have a cloud of interstellar matter with a density of about 10,000 gas molecules per cubic centimeter. That's very, very little compared with the concentration of gases in Earth's atmosphere, which contain millions of molecules in every cubic centimeter. But it's a lot denser than the thinly scattered matter in most of the interstellar medium. The cloud is dark. It does not shine—yet. It is extremely cold, about 10 to 50 Kelvin (about −440 to −370°F, −263 to −223°C). Clumps of matter form cloud cores where gravitational collapse begins. Some regions of the cloud may be of higher density.

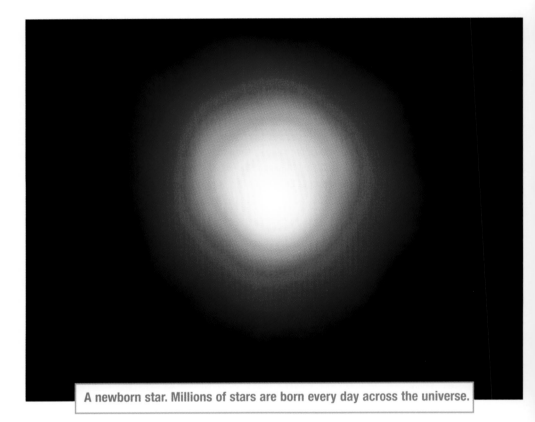

A newborn star. Millions of stars are born every day across the universe.

Shock waves from supernovae may cause high-pressure regions or magnetic fields may help concentrate particles in some way. Most of these soon dissipate but sometimes they may last long enough to gather more material by gravitational attraction. This, in turn, may attract more—so there is a runaway effect and large amounts of matter start to funnel into the cloud core. As the material spirals inward, it starts to speed up (as skaters speed up when they hug their arms close to their bodies) and the temperature increases.

Gravity builds and the cloud core finally collapses as matter pours into the center. Pressure increases at the center. Temperature rises, and by this time, more matter falls into the center, causing further rises in temperature. As the temperature soars, energy begins to radiate from the surface.

In the beginning, the rotation is probably very, very slow—the motion possibly inherited from the turbulence of the cloud out of which it was born. Meanwhile, the core becomes denser and denser, its mass grows to the dimension of a star, and the rotation speed increases.

Early in this process, newly forming stars, called protostars, are hidden away from view amid the dust of the nebula from which they took

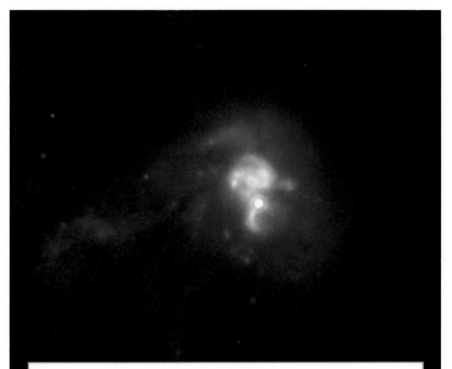

This is a color composite of what scientists term an ultraluminous infrared galaxy. Such galaxies glow extremely brightly in infrared light. This particular galaxy is producing about 200 stars like our Sun every year. The yellow region at center is where these stars are being born.

form. They cannot be seen by regular, optical telescopes—only infrared and radio telescopes can detect them. Eventually, though, after about a million years, the protostar transforms into an infant star, known as a T Tauri star (named after the first one astronomers ever found).

Young Stars

Images of the nebula NGC 604, an enormous cloud of gas and dust located in the galaxy M33 about 3 million light years away from Earth, definitely show that stars are being born there. In this vast

This is the NGC 604 Nebula, captured here by the *Hubble Space Telescope* but first discovered in 1784 by William Herschel. The nebula is home to more than 200 stars that are much larger than our Sun.

These unusual pillarlike structures are columns of interstellar hydrogen gas in the Eagle Nebula, where new stars are being formed.

nursery, researchers estimate more than 200 young stars exist that are 15 to 60 times the mass of our Sun. The nebula is illuminated by their radiation as they glow within its cloudy mass like hundreds of bright candles.

The spectacular Eagle Nebula (M16), about 7,000 light years away, also harbors emerging new stars. The striking columns or stalks that reach out from this nebula show regions known as EGGs (evaporating gaseous globules) near the tips of the stalks. Astronomers sus-

The Brown Dwarf: Not Quite a Star

Among stars and planets, brown dwarfs are somewhere in between—too massive to be planets and too small to make star status. They never became massive enough for nuclear reactions to kick into action in their cores. At the same time, they are much more massive than Jupiter, the largest planet in our solar system. Jupiter's composition is starlike, and it gives off a faint energy. At one time scientists speculated that Jupiter was on its way to becoming part of a binary system

At right is an infrared Hubble image of a swarm of newborn brown dwarf stars. Brown dwarfs are small stars whose mass is not great enough to allow them to fuse hydrogen and shine steadily. Instead, they fade and cool as they grow older. In visible light (at left), the brown dwarfs are too dim to be seen.

pect that these regions contain star nurseries. The fingerlike formations of the stalks are anchored in a huge cloud of cold hydrogen. The columns themselves (referred to as "elephant trunks") have diameters measuring several *light years* across. They are at least a light year in length and they are filled with dense, cool gases. These gases may be dense enough to collapse on themselves—the beginning stages of star with the Sun. (Many stars come in pairs, called binary stars, and orbit around each other. This arrangement is so common in the universe, that many scientists have speculated about the existence of a "companion star" to our Sun.) However, Jupiter is much too small for nuclear fusion to take place in its core. Its mass is from 20 to 50 times less than the smallest brown dwarfs—and even they lack the mass for nuclear fusion.

If no thermonuclear fusion is taking place inside brown dwarfs and gas giants like Jupiter, you may ask, how can they give off any energy at all? Why do they generate even a faint light? Scientists have found that Jupiter generates heat in its core, produced by the immense pressure of its mass pressing inward, with gas molecules colliding and jostling, causing friction and releasing energy. Because much of Jupiter's mass is fluid, some form of partial convection takes place, carrying the heat from Jupiter's core to the surface gases of its atmosphere, and releasing it in the form of light (visible to optical telescopes) and heat (visible with

infrared). Most scientists also say that deep within its core a brown dwarf burns deuterium, the same rare form of hydrogen that plays an important part in fusion. Like Jupiter, the brown dwarf does not get hot enough to enter fusion, but it does generate heat and also has full convection processes running the energy to the surface where it is released—both visibly and in the infrared.

Brown dwarfs are difficult to see because they, like Jupiter, do not really shine much at all. The first brown dwarf ever discovered was found in 1995 in the constellation Lepus (the hare), located in the Southern Hemisphere near Orion and Columba. It was the first one found in 20 years of looking. Astronomers used infrared detectors and telescopes at Palomar Observatory to find the brown dwarf's faint light, and then discovery was confirmed by an image taken by the *Hubble Space Telescope*. Called G1229B, the brown dwarf gives off about 1 percent of the radiation of the smallest known star—even though it may be as much as 50 times as massive as Jupiter.

formation. Infrared images of these regions show contracting, warming dust clouds. These clouds are on their way to becoming stars.

Young Stars with Young Families

Hubble has also captured visual proof that young stars are commonly surrounded by a flat, pancake-shaped disk. These disks contain the raw material for the formation of planets, so astronomers expect to find planets around quite a few other stars besides our Sun. In fact, they already have found evidence of many other planetary systems. *Hubble* researchers have also noticed that jets of gas are expelled from the centers of the same disks of dust and gas where very young stars have been found.

Getting a New Look at Stars

The life and death of stars has become a subject of growing interest among astronomers since the beginning of the twentieth century. Ever-imposing instruments and spaceborne observatories have enabled scientists to witness these complex evolutionary processes as never before. The *Hubble Space Telescope* and the *Chandra X-ray Telescope* have documented many colorful details and made these vistas accessible to everyone, as well.

For example, *Hubble*'s infrared camera has captured an image of an enormously luminous star known as the "Pistol Star," named after the shape of the nebula around it. This star lies about 25,000 light years away, near the center of the Milky Way. Large quantities of interstellar dust hide many of its features. However, it is 10 million times more luminous than our Sun. It would take the Sun nearly four months to emit as much energy as the Pistol Star does in one second! The Pistol Star is mammoth, so big it could fill the entire diameter of Earth's orbit, swallowing up most of the inner solar system. The dust is so thick around it, though, that no optical telescope would ever see it. The Pistol Star is visible only by using the infrared camera.

If this star were an automobile, it would be a gas guzzler. Stars this massive put out so much radiation that they eat up all their fuel in a

The British astronomer William Herschel discovered the Eskimo Nebula in 1787, but it was not until after *Hubble* was serviced in late 1999 that the world was treated to an image like this. This planetary nebula, NGC 2392, is also sometimes referred to the "clown's face nebula."

short time and burn out quickly. Often the end is violent and dramatic. Astronomers think that the Pistol Star will shed its mass in a series of ever-violent explosions in about 1 to 3 million years.

The *Hubble Space Telescope* captured this image of the Pistol Star in October 1997. Before Hubble, the Pistol Star was obscured by dust, but now scientists know that it emits 10 million more times the light of the Sun and is 100 times more massive. It is so huge that it threw off the mass that makes up the Pistol Nebula, which surrounds it in this image.

The gas nebula around the Pistol Star shows that it already has seen some violence. In fact, eruptions in the outer layers of the star may have created the nebula at the outset. Where did a star this massive come from—and why is it so much more luminous than other stars? Possibly the Pistol Star is not just one star—but several. Only more study will tell.

Another star, Eta Carinae, located 8,000 light years away, is a superstar surrounded by an enormous gas nebula. This superstar, or supergiant, is 4 million times more luminous than the Sun and it is 100 times as massive—one of the most massive in the galaxy. If Eta Carnae were as close as the nearest star, you could read by its light. Astronomers estimate that Eta Carinae will explode in a violent supernova soon—in as few as 100,000 years. (This may not be soon in terms of a human lifetime, but on the astronomical scale it's very soon.) Finally, after the supernova, it will end its life as a black hole or a neutron star.

Eta Carinae is visible only from the Southern Hemisphere, near the Southern Cross. Since 1677, when astronomer Edmond Halley cataloged it, it became brighter, then much brighter, faded briefly, and after that grew steadily brighter. It reached its peak in April 1843, becoming the second-brightest star in the sky, after Sirius. It put out as much light as about 5 million Suns. Ejected matter from Eta Carinae during this bright period caused its light to fade to observers on Earth, and this "dust storm" has only expanded just enough to let the star's brightness show through again.

Hubble was able to obtain a clear picture of Eta Carinae, thanks to image-processing techniques. Many interesting features are visible in the matter ejected by this energetic star, including two large polar clouds that streak out into space at a rate of 400 miles (650 km) per second. Ultraviolet light emerges more from the equatorial region of the star, since it is not as thick with dust that absorbs the UV radiation. The polar clouds are redder. Astronomers also have noted dust lobes, condensations, and radial streaks in this image. They can even recognize structures within the lobes and trace their evolution.

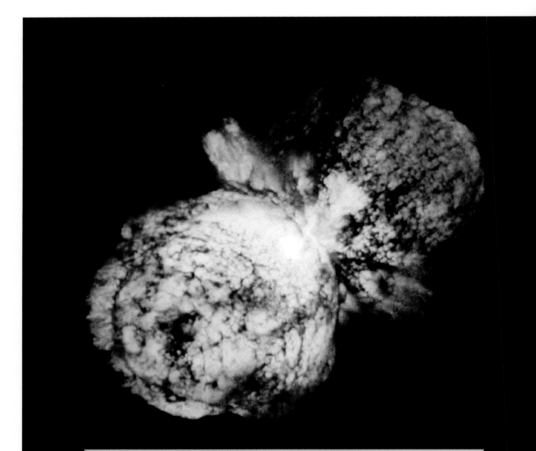

Eta Carinae is a super-massive star that erupted about 150 years ago, blowing off massive amounts of material that formed into two large lobes along the star's polar axis. The massive flow of gas blocks part of the view, but the star—or possibly two stars—linking the lobes remain among the largest and most luminous stars in the Galaxy.

Using two images of Eta Carinae and its nebula taken at different times, scientists have shown how furiously this pair of gas and dust clouds is expanding. By comparing X-ray, optical, infrared, and radio images, scientists have begun to piece together some of this huge star's history. During the eruption period that took place 150 years ago, Eta Carinae must have lost a mass of matter equivalent to the Sun's entire mass or more. Most was lost at the star's equator, with the rest speeding away at the star's poles. The thrown-off matter was so thick, it hid the star from view—which is why it seemed so much dimmer. However, scientists have also noticed that the star changes its spectrum every 5.5 years or so, and experiences waves of increased X-ray emission every 85 days. The meaning of these patterns is not yet certain, but some researchers think that Eta Carinae is actually a binary system (two stars orbiting each other) with an orbit that is completed every 5.5 years. If this is true, Eta Carinae is the most massive binary system ever discovered.

Lasting for billions of years, a star will emit a steady amount of light and heat during its main sequence of life.

Chapter 4

Midlife: The Main Sequence

he main thing to remember about the life patterns of stars—their evolution—is that every step of a star's development takes place under the influence of the force of its own gravity. It is constantly trying to make itself smaller. During its life cycle, various other forces overcome the gravitational force for periods of time. However, a star either is always in the process of shrinking or is temporarily paused in the process of shrinking.

Star life begins when the infant star collapses out of the constantly stirring mixture of interstellar dust and gas. Nuclear fusion begins, and the conversion of hydrogen to helium creates a great counterpressure to the shrinking caused by gravity. This is the protostar stage. Protostars evolve into mature stars that are typically known as "Main Sequence" stars. The squeeze comes to a stop and the star becomes stable as it begins its life.

However, stars of different masses have different life stories, with variations in luminosity and temperature, even among main sequence stars. Stars having only a tenth of the Sun's mass end up much cooler than the Sun, and much dimmer—about 3,000 K or less—and about half as bright. A star having three times the Sun's mass is twice as bright as the Sun and, at 12,000 K, about twice as hot. For all these, the main sequence follows—the longest period in a star's life stages. Like human beings, stars change the least during their "adult" years, their midlife, which in most stars lasts for billions of years. The process of changing just 0.01 percent of the Sun's mass into sunshine takes a billion years, and light, cool, dim stars live many billions of years. They consume their hydrogen in a leisurely timeframe. These stars, known as red dwarfs, are the oldest and most numerous of the Main Sequence stars. Massive, hot, highly luminous stars, though, are a completely different story. A blue giant star, for example, consumes all the hydrogen in its core in just a few million years. In astronomical terms, that is just a blink of an eye, and then it's nearly all over. Compared with the midlife, rapid changes took place as the star formed—and once the hydrogen fuel begins to run out, the changes will become more rapid again. In the meantime, as fuel in the core is used up, the rate of consumption increases, and the star's luminosity stays steady for a time.

However, after a while the temperature keeps increasing, and the outer layers of the core expand into the star's outer layers. There, additional hydrogen becomes available to the fusion in the core, so that over time, luminosity slowly increases. Five billion years ago, shortly after its birth, our Sun was smaller, redder, and cooler.

Then the outward pressure of the heat produced by the core's nuclear reactions no longer balances the gravitational attraction that creates inward pressure. The core shrinks; then the temperature rises and the star brightens, releasing such a huge amount of energy that it swells like an enormous balloon. In the coming 5 billion years, the Sun will change faster. Finally, when the Sun's core contains no more hydrogen fuel, our star will be 75 percent larger and two times brighter than it is today. Eventually, billions of years from now, the Sun will swell enormously. The outer envelope will expand, and the temperature will drop. It may increase as much as 100 times its present size and its outer layers may push out as far as the orbit of Mercury. This is the red giant stage, the last stage before the beginning of the end.

The outer layers continue expanding outward. Meanwhile, the core is completely out of hydrogen fuel, and only helium remains. The helium core begins shrinking until it is about the size of our planet. The density increases, and the interior temperature rises to about 100 million degrees K. It is the beginning of the end of a red giant's days.

The shock waves from the explosion of a star in the Cygnus constellation some 15,000 years ago collide with stationary gas clouds to create the brilliant array of color known as the Cygnus loop.

Chapter 5

How
Stars Die

R ed giants end their days one of several ways, depending upon their mass and the elements formed at their core: It may become a white dwarf or a supergiant, or it may go supernova and leave behind either a neutron star or a black hole.

When the hydrogen fuel finally runs out in the core of a star, it begins the final stages of its evolution. By now all the hydrogen has been converted to helium, and the star's core consists of nearly pure helium. The production of energy by the nuclear forces slows and dies away. Expansion stops and gravity takes over. The core contracts, as it did before, during the star's youth. Now the nuclear process causes further fusion. Helium fuses to carbon, giving off more energy. The contraction stops, but not for long. When the helium fuel is gone, contraction begins again.

What happens next? That depends on the mass of the star. For stars like our Sun, the once-mighty star shrinks to about the size and mass of Earth. Nuclear fusion has ended. Gravity is held off by properties of the star's atomic particles, and the star ends up as a stable ball of carbon and oxygen, a white dwarf star.

Stars with more mass are another story, however. These stars reach higher temperatures and have greater densities than stars like the Sun, barely maintaining any fusion processes. Nuclear fusion continues, using up each new fuel as it is produced, giving off energy, then contracting again, until finally it is a dense ball of iron.

Our Sun's Future: White Dwarf

A main sequence "G" star—an average star such as the Sun—will most likely end its red-giant phase by throwing off its outer layers, forming a shell of glowing gas called a planetary nebula (even though it has nothing to do with planets). Sometimes this process is so violent it is considered a type of supernova. The star itself becomes a *white dwarf*—a very small, dense, hot star caught in a stable, almost unending stage. It is about the size of a planet, but its mass is the same as a normal star—so its density is enormous. About 1 the stars in our Galaxy are white dwarfs. Because they a

This is planetary nebula Mz3, also known as the Ant Nebula, as seen by *Hubble*. The reason for the nebula's unusual shape still puzzles scientists, who are especially interested in Mz3 because its central star closely resembles our sun.

are not very luminous and are not easily detected. Gravity has done its job and has packed the core's electrons and protons tightly together. On Earth, a spoonful of this material would weigh several tons.

Over time, white dwarfs grow cooler and fade and shrink smaller and smaller. The smallest known white dwarf is van Maanen's Star. Its diameter is only 7,800 miles (12,550 km)—slightly smaller than Earth. Eventually, a white dwarf becomes a dark, cool remnant, the forseeable fate of our Sun some 5 billion to 7 billion years from now.

Antares is a type of star known as a red giant, which means that its mass is increasing as it uses up its fuel.

Supergiants

A very massive star begins to expand greatly once it has used up all its hydrogen fuel. As it expands, it cools, forming the largest known type of star, the supergiant. These are the largest and most luminous of all the stars—dying stars with a diameter as great as 1,000 times the diameter of the Sun. A couple of examples are Antares (with a diameter 330 times the Sun's) and Betelgeuse (with a changing diameter between 375 and 595 times the diameter of the Sun).

Supernova!

A supernova is a giant, cataclysmic explosion of a supergiant star. This happens when the core of a star that is especially high in mass has gone as far as it can under nuclear forces. Then, suddenly, it collapses. Stored gravitational energy is released in a giant burst and the star explodes, violently and spectacularly. It may give off light as bright as

Cassiopeia A is the remnant left by a violent supernova. The explosion was first observed by the Danish astronomer Tycho Brahe in 1572, but today's deep-space imagery provides a view that he could only have dreamed of.

100 million Suns—or even brighter. A supernova may appear as bright as a small galaxy in the sky. These hugh explosions may occur in a galaxy about once every 100 years. All this happens very quickly, and a new star seems to appear in the sky.

Such an explosion must have occurred in 1054, when the appearance of a new star was written into astronomical record in China and all over the world. It created the formation called the Crab Nebula, the leftovers from the explosion, an enormous cloud of gas, rapidly

This image of the Crab Nebula was taken by the *Chandra X-Ray Telescope*. Now cataloged as M1, the Crab Nebula is the remnant of a supernova that Chinese astronomers observed in 1054. It was probably the same explosion recorded at that time by the Anasazi Indians of present-day Arizona and New Mexico.

expanding and cooling. At its center, a pulsar—a spinning neutron star—is believed to be the remnant of the exploded star.

People often get confused between a nova and a supernova. A nova is just a star puffing off gases in the more or less normal course of its life process, and then the star reduces in brightness and goes more or less back to life as it was before, as Eta Carinae has done. A supernova is the climatic, violent conclusion of the life of a supergiant star.

After the Explosion: Neutron Stars and Black Holes

A supernova leaves behind one or two remnants—depending upon how much mass remains. If a mass about three times the size of the Sun is left over after the blast, the remains become a neutron star. If more than three times the mass of the Sun is left, the star collapses and becomes a black hole.

Neutron Star

Soviet physicist Lev Landau first put forth the concept in 1932 that a very high-density form of matter might exist. Two American physicists, Walter Baade and Fritz Zwicky, came up with the idea two years later that such a substance might form during a supernova.

Since then, astronomers have discovered neutron stars—the tiniest of stars, yet "superdense." That is, their atoms have been squeezed together so tightly by the star's collapse that electrons and protons have combined to form neutrons. (That's why it's called a "neutron" star.) A neutron star may actually have a diameter of only 12 miles (20 km)—with a mass as great as the Sun's! Or, put another way, the neutrons that make up a neutron star are so tightly packed together that a piece the size of a sugar cube would have as much mass as Earth's entire human population of some 6 billion people.

Supernovae are fascinating in themselves. However, they also can serve as a handy yardstick for measuring the size of the universe. To obtain an accurate measurement, though, researchers have to catch a supernova early, before it reaches its brightest stages. Only about a dozen supernovae have been spied by astronomers in their early stages. Recently, though, astronomers found success in catching supernovae as much as two weeks before they reach their greatest brightness. They spotted supernova 2002 DJ in June 2002 in the nearby galaxy NGC 5018, still in its very first stages.

The earlier astronomers detect the stellar explosion, the easier it is to find out the star's original chemical composition from its spectrum—its characteristic mix of light and energy given off in the blast. At the very beginning, the elements seen in the spectrum are largely the original material of the white dwarf star. The explosion typically continues for weeks or more, and astronomers have usually spied the event late in its process. By then, the material has become fused together to form new substances and the original makeup of the star is no longer easy to determine.

White dwarf stars consistently die when their mass reaches 1.4 times that of the Sun. This maximum mass for white dwarfs is known as the Chandrasekhar limit. So white dwarf stars almost always have the same mass when they go supernova—and the amount of energy and light given off by the explosion is almost always the same. So, by measuring the luminosity, or brightness, of the explosion as seen from Earth, cosmologists can tell how far away it is.

Supernova 2002 DJ took place 130 million light years away. That is, it hap-

Researchers think that, unlike the gaseous surface of most stars, neutrons have a solid crust at the surface, possibly composed of iron in crystalline form. Beneath the crust lies a solid shell rich in neutrons, and the core may be made up of superfluid material. Observers believe that small changes in the neutron's structure—starquakes—may account for irregularities in its period of rotation.

The stripped and superdense core of a once great star ends its days peacefully. Stable and no longer stormy, this strange object about the size of a small city is no longer torn by violent forces.

pened 130 million years ago. Would its composition be the same, though, as a white dwarf that is 10 billion light years away? It would be far older—nearly 10 billion years older! So the older star would represent a much earlier stage in the evolution of the universe. Cosmologists need to know what differences in composition exist between recently developed stars and those that evolved long, long ago. Only then can they be certain of their measurements. When they have collected enough early data from both old and recent supernovae, they will begin to have a much more accurate picture of the size of the universe and its aging process.

A white dwarf is what becomes of a star like our Sun when it exhausts its thermonuclear fuel, casts off much of its mass, and begins the long process of cooling. In this *HST* image, the white dwarf is the bright pinpoint of light at the very center of the image, surrounded by planetary nebula NGC 2440.

Yet not all neutron stars are completely quiet. In 1967 a team of radio astronomers in England found something strange. Jocelyn Bell Burnell and Antony Hewish were working with a big radio antenna they had built, when they noticed a new kind of pulsing signal. Its source became known as a pulsar. The term "pulsar" is an abbreviation for "pulsating radio star." Today, most researchers think that pulsars are actually rotating neutron stars. The rapid rotation, they think, causes the emission of radio waves brought about by the movement of charged particles at its magnetic poles. A pulsar exists in the constellation Vela (part of Argo), in the Southern Hemisphere.

Black Hole

Just a few years ago, many astronomers thought of black holes as theoretical. However, recent discoveries make black holes far more likely than anyone once thought. The trouble is, a black hole is a defunct star that is so massive it lets nothing escape, including light. So, of course, you can't see them. Some people have compared looking for black holes with looking for a black cat in a darkened basement.

Black holes, scientists believe, are the very last stage for extremely massive stars—having 10 to 15 times the mass of the Sun. During a supernova, the exploding star throws off its outer layers. The remaining core gets denser and denser, collapsing inward. Finally, the star's entire mass is packed into a small, infinitely dense space. All the star's matter is packed into a tiny, single point at the center. In physics, such a point is called a singularity—and theorists believe that this point is smaller than the nucleus of an atom. That's small!

A black hole has such enormous gravitational force that nothing can escape its spherical boundary, known as an *event horizon*. The radius of the event horizon is used to measure the size of a black hole, and black holes are detected by their effect—since they do not reflect light, and they do not emit light. (Nothing, not even light, can pass the event horizon.) Evidence for as many as seven black holes have been found in the Milky Way and nearby galaxies with the help of the *Hubble Space Telescope* and the *Chandra X-Ray Observatory*. Intense X rays coming from a region may indicate the presence of either a neutron star or a black hole. When a neutron star has newly formed from the dense remnants of a supernova, it spits out high-energy particles that produce X rays over the course of several thousand years. Even an old neutron star may also produce X rays when matter from a nearby

The *Chandra X-ray Telescope* captured this image of the galaxy Centaurus A. The greenish material at the center of the image are jets of high-energy particles being blasted away from a black hole at the galaxy's nucleus.

star falls onto its surface. X-ray telescopes also can provide an unequaled view of superheated matter that is swirling toward the event horizon of a black hole. X-ray data from these two space observatories have detected evidence of small amounts of energy visible just before they become absorbed, presumably by the event horizon of a black hole. None of this is yet absolute proof, but it's close.

Recycling Old Star Dust

From the star dust left in the wake of a great star's explosive death, new stars are born. The final explosions that end some stars live's blow helium and other elements out into the interstellar medium. The dust combines with interstellar gas. Soon dust and gas begin to clump together. Clumps of dust and gas fall inward toward an ever-growing center. The center becomes denser and its mass becomes larger. Soon, fusion begins, the clump begins to shine, and a new star is born. The cycle begins all over again.

So ends this account of the life and death of stars—but it is really only the beginning. Much more is already known than could fit in this book. And with every passing day scientists make new discoveries and gain new insights from space telescopes and mountaintop observatories; from measurements, calculations, and observations; and from computer modeling, to name just a few of the astrophysicists bag of tricks for uncovering the mysteries of the universe. Much more remains to discover and understand about these vastly diverse and fascinating far-off objects of the cosmos.

Missions to "Our Star," the Sun

Vital Statistics

Spacecraft	Type of Mission	Year of Launch	Sponsor
Pioneer 5	Solar Orbiter	1959	NASA
Pioneer 6	Solar Orbiter	1965	NASA
Pioneer 7	Solar Orbiter	1966	NASA
Pioneer 8	Solar Orbiter	1967	NASA
Pioneer 9	Solar Orbiter	1968	NASA
Skylab	Space Station/Solar Observatory; Earth orbit	1973	NASA
Explorer 49	Lunar Orbiter; Solar Observer	1973	NASA
Helios 1	Solar Orbiter	1974	NASA/West Germany
Helios 2	Solar Orbiter	1976	NASA/West Germany
Solar Maximum Mission (SMM)	Solar Orbiter	1980	NASA
Ulysses	South-North Solar Orbiter	1990	NASA/ESA

Spacecraft	Type of Mission	Year of Launch	Sponsor
YOHKOH	Solar Orbiter	1991	Japan, United States, and United Kingdom
SOLAR AND HELIOSPHERIC OBSERVATORY (SOHO)	Solar Orbiter/Observatory	1995	ESA/NASA
ADVANCED COMPOSITION EXPLORER (ACE)	Solar Orbiter	1997	NASA
(TRANSITION REGION AND CORONAL EXPLORER) TRACE	Solar Orbiter	1998	NASA

Studying the Stars: A Timeline

1814 — Joseph von Fraunhofer observes dark lines in the spectrum cast by solar light.

1842 — Christian Johann Doppler discovers that the shift in a star's spectrum indicates movement of the star.

1859 — Gustav Kirchhoff and Robert Bunsen show the significance of Fraunhofer's lines and establish the composition of the Sun and other stars as primarily hydrogen.

1907 — Albert Einstein first publishes his equation $e=mc^2$.

1924 — Edwin P. Hubble discovers that there are more galaxies in the universe than our own Milky Way. He also determines, with Milton Humason, that the galaxies are moving away from each other and that the universe is expanding.

1959 — *Pioneer 5* solar monitor is launched into solar orbit; space probe remains in solar orbit 41 years later.

1965 — *Pioneer 6* solar probe is launched; was still sending information from solar orbit 35 years later.

1966	*Pioneer 7* solar probe is launched.
1967	*Pioneer 8* solar probe is launched by the United States; was still sending information from solar orbit 33 years later.
1968	*Pioneer 9* solar probe is launched into solar orbit.
1973	*Skylab*, the first U.S. space station, is launched. Between 1973 and 1974, it is staffed by three crews for a total of 171 days. Astronauts took more than 150,000 images of the Sun.
	The United States launches the *Explorer 49* solar probe to examine solar physics from orbit around the Moon.
1974	*Helios 1* solar probe is launched by the United States and West Germany and is inserted into solar orbit; the mission lasts until 1975.
1976	*Helios 2* solar probe is launched by the United States and West Germany; its orbit comes within 26.72 million miles (43 million km) of the Sun.

1977	Congress approves funding for a sophisticated space telescope, the first of NASA's Great Observatories, later named the *Hubble Space Telescope* (*HST*).
1979	NASA begins building the *HST*.
	Skylab reenters Earth's atmosphere.
1980	The *Solar Maximum Mission (SMM)* is launched by the United States to study the Sun during the active part of the solar cycle; the mission lasts until 1989.
1990	*Ulysses* spacecraft launched by the United States and the European Space Agency (ESA) to study both the north and south polar regions of the Sun.
	The *Hubble Space Telescope* is launched from the space shuttle *Discovery*.
1991	The *Compton Gamma-Ray Observatory (CGRO)* is launched from the space shuttle *Atlantis*.

Yohkoh solar probe is launched by Japan, the United States, and the United Kingdom to study high-energy radiation from solar flares.

1995 — *SOHO* (*Solar and Heliospheric Observatory*), a ESA-NASA mission to the Sun, is launched by ESA.

Ulysses makes first pass by the north pole of the Sun.

1997 — *ACE* (*Advanced Composition Explorer*) is launched by the United States into orbit about 932,000 miles (1.5 million km) from Earth to observe galaxies, the solar wind, and the Sun.

1998 — *TRACE* (*Transition Region and Coronal Explorer*) is launched by the United States to study the upper atmosphere of the Sun.

1999 — *TRACE* begins mission.

Chandra X-ray Observatory, another part of NASA's Great Observatories series, is launched aboard the space shuttle *Columbia*, and put into orbit.

2010 — (Planned) James Webb Space Telescope (NGST or "Hubble 2") to be launched.

Glossary

axis—the imaginary line running from pole to pole through a planet's center. A planet spins, or rotates, along its axis.

binary stars—a pair of stars

black dwarf—a star at the end of its evolution, when it has completely exhausted its fuel and is cold, small, dense, and dark (not the same as a black hole)

brown dwarf—a "failed star" that does not have enough mass to produce fusion but is almost large enough to be a star

black hole—an area in space, possibly a defunct star, where mass has become so dense that its gravitational pull cannot be escaped; once an object, even light, has fallen into the black hole, it cannot emerge. (See *event horizon*.)

composition—what something—such as the Sun or a star—is made of

constellations—the arrangement of groups of stars

convection—the rapid movement of materials as a result of unevenly distributed temperature; heat generally causes a material to expand, becoming less dense, so it rises; cold causes a material to condense, becoming denser and heavier, causing it to fall or move downward *core*—the distinct region that is located at the center of a star, planet, or other object in space

cycle—a single execution of a series of patterns or events that repeats on a regular schedule

density—how much of a substance exists in a given volume

diameter—the distance in a straight line through the center of a sphere, such as the Sun or a planet

$e = mc^2$—Albert Einstein's most famous equation. It states that energy (e) is equivalent to mass (m) multiplied times the speed of light squared. The speed of light is a constant (c)—always the same at 186,000 miles (299,338 km) per second.

eject—throw upward and outward

electromagnetic radiation—energy transmitted through space in the form of waves; each kind of electromagnetic radiation has a different wavelength, or frequency, and all kinds of electromagnetic radiation travel at the speed of light

electromagnetic spectrum—the full range of the waves and frequencies of electromagnetic radiation. The Sun gives off electro-

magnetic radiation, and sunlight makes up the portion of the spectrum that you can see. You can use a prism to break visible light up into its parts, including red, yellow, green, blue, and violet light.

event horizon—the region surrounding a black hole from which nothing, not even light, can escape

frequency—number of complete oscillations per second of energy in the form of waves, for example electromagnetic radiation or radio waves

galaxy—a large system of gas, dust, and millions or billions of stars

the Galaxy—the Milky Way; the galaxy that includes our solar system. Scientists use a capital "G" to set this galaxy apart from all others.

gravity—the force of attraction between two objects with mass—the larger the mass and the closer the object, the stronger the force of gravity

heliosphere—the region in space that is influenced by the Sun

infrared rays—radiation just beyond visible red, having longer wavelengths; infrared rays are invisible to human eyes

interstellar medium—matter found in regions between stars

ion— a charged (either negative or positive) atomic particle

light year—the distance light travels in one year, about 5.88 trillion miles (9.46 trillion km)

local group—the group of nearby galaxies in our Galaxy (the Milky Way), the Andromeda Galaxy (M31), and about three dozen others.

magnitude—the brightness of a stars organized into six different levels

mass—the amount of material a body contains

molecular cloud—very cold, huge collections of molecules that represent the building blocks of life and the universe, including carbon, hydrogen, oxygen, nitrogen, and other atoms joined together in amino acids, proteins, and other substances; molecular clouds are the most massive objects in the Milky Way, up to one million times more massive than the Sun.

neutrino—a tiny subatomic particle having no mass and no charge, released during nuclear fusion

neutron star—a dying star that has collapsed in on itself and has become packed so tightly that it has become extremely dense

nova—a binary star that brightens because material from its partner has spilled onto its exterior

nuclear fusion—the reaction that takes place when light atomic nuclei combine to form a heavier nucleus with the release of energy

nucleus, nuclei (pl.)—the central portion of an atom; it is composed of protons, or protons and neutrons, carries a positive charge, and contains nearly all of the atom's mass.

orbit—the path an object, such as a planet, travels as it revolves around another body, such as the Sun

optical telescope—a telescope that works in the visible light (what we can see with our eyes region of the spectrum).

parallax—the apparent shift in a star when it is viewed from two different positions on Earth

photon—a tiny packet of electromagnetic energy—that is, a piece of light. A photon has no mass, no charge, and an unknown lifetime.

plasma—ionized gas

proper motion—motion of the stars traveling at right angle to the observer's line of sight

protostar—a very young star, at the beginning of its formation

pulsars—neutron stars that send out a pulsing stream of radio signals

red giant—an old star that has swelled up in size, increasing vastly in size; its surface is relatively cool, and it gives off a red glow.

revolution—one complete tour in an orbit around the Sun

revolve—to move in a path, or orbit, around another object. Earth revolves around the Sun, making a complete trip in one year.

rotate—to turn or spin around an axis

rotation—one complete turn of an object in space on its axis

solar nebula—a primitive cloud of gas and material from which the Sun and the planets were born

spectrum—a series of colors formed when white light (sunlight or starlight) is passed through a prism to break the light up into its parts. Since the discovery of invisible electromagnetic radiation (such as

infrared and UV rays) beyond visible red andviolet, the term has been extended to include these invisible rays as well, which can be detected using a spectroscope.

supernova—extremely bright explosion of a very large star, reaching extraordinarily high luminosity up to one billion times that of the Sun

T Tauri star—A protostar that is blowing off dust and is on the verge of moving into the adult star (Main Sequence) phase.

ultraviolet (UV) rays—"black light," the type of radiation with wavelengths just shorter than violet light; UV rays are invisible to humans

vacuum—an absence of any gases

visible light—the portion of the electromagnetic spectrum that we can see

volume—the amount of space occupied by an object, expressed in three-dimensional terms

wave—the form taken by electromagnetic radiation, having simultaneous periodic variations of electric and magnetic field intensity and that include radio waves, infrared, visible light, ultraviolet, X rays, and gamma rays

wavelength—the distance between peaks of a wave

white dwarf—an old star, toward the end of its evolution, often white, usually very dense, small, and faint

The news from space changes fast, so it's always a good idea to check the copyright date on books, CD-ROMs, and videotapes to make sure that you are getting up-to-date information. One good place to look for current information from NASA is U.S. government depository libraries. There are several in each state.

Books

Campbell, Ann Jeanette. *The New York Public Library Amazing Space: A Book of Answers for Kids.* New York: John Wiley & Sons, 1997.

Estalella, Robert, and Marcel Socias. *Our Star—The Sun.* Hauppauge, N.Y.: Barron's Educational Series, Inc., 1993.

Gallant, Roy A. *When the Sun Dies.* New York: Marshall Cavendish, Inc., 1998.

Kosek, Jane Kelly. *What's Inside the Sun?* New York: The Rosen Publishing Group, Inc., 1999.

Lippincott, Kristen. *Astronomy (Eyewitness Science).* New York: Dorling Kindersley Publishing, Inc., 1994.

Melton, Melanie. *Will Black Holes Devour the Universe? and 100 Other Questions and Answers about Astronomy, from the publishers of Astronomy Magazine.* Waukesha, WI: Kalmbach Publishing, 1994.

Mitton, Simon and Jacqueline. *The Young Oxford Book of Astronomy.* New York: Oxford University Press, 1995.

Mitton, Jacqueline. *Young Oxford Library of Science: Stars and Planets.* New York: Oxford University Press, 2002.

Spangenburg, Ray, and Kit Moser. *The Hubble Space Telescope.* Danbury, Conn.: Franklin Watts, 2002.

————. *Observing the Universe.* Danbury, Conn.: Franklin Watts, 2003.

Organizations and Online Sites

These organizations and groups are good sources of information about the Sun, the stars, and the universe. Many of the online sites listed below are NASA sites, with links to many other interesting sources of information about stars and their life cycles. You can also sign up to receive NASA news on many subjects via e-mail.

Astronomical Society of the Pacific
http://www.astrosociety.org/
390 Ashton Avenue
San Francisco, CA 94112
Organization devoted to expanding knowledge about the universe and astronomy

Hubble Site

http://hubble.stsci.edu/

A gallery of stunning images of star formation and a wealth of information about *Hubble* are provided on the Public Outreach site for the *Hubble Space Telescope*. The site is produced by the Space Telescope Science Institute, which manages *Hubble* and the *James Webb Space Telescope*, to be launched in 2010 as the successor to *HST*.

NASA Ask a Space Scientist

http://image.gsfc.nasa.gov/poetry/ask/askmag.html#list

Interactive page where NASA scientists answer your questions about astronomy, space, and space missions. Also has archives and fact sheets.

Sky Online

http://www.skyandtelescope.com

The Web site for *Sky and Telescope* magazine and other publications of Sky Publishing Corporation. This site has a good weekly news section on general space and astronomy news. The site also contains many good tips for amateur astronomers, as well as a nice selection of links. A list of science museums, planetariums, and astronomy clubs organized by state helps locate nearby places to visit, as well.

Solar and Heliospheric Observatory (SOHO) Mission

http://sohowww.nascom.nasa.gov/

Official site of the *SOHO* mission, a joint ESA/NASA mission to study the Sun's internal structure. *SOHO*'s observations have also helped scientists understand other stars.

Ulysses Mission

http://ulysses.jpl.nasa.gov/

Official NASA site for information concerning the *Ulysses* mission and its discoveries about the Sun (and other stars).

Windows to the Universe

http://windows.ucar.edu/

Visit the links here for news about the universe: recent discoveries, images, constellations, the night sky, stars, nebulae, exotic objects, galaxies, and the structure of the universe. This NASA site, developed by the University of Michigan, also includes sections on "Our Planet," "Our Solar System," "Space Missions," and "Kids' Space." Choose from presentation levels of beginner, intermediate, or advanced.

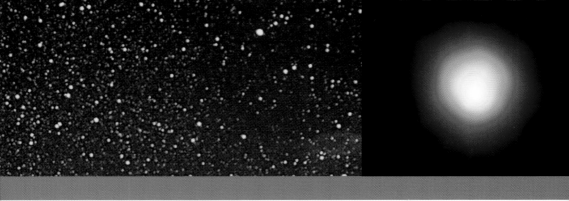

About the Authors

Ray Spangenburg and **Kit Moser** are a husband-and-wife writing team specializing in science and technology. They have written over 50 books and more than 100 articles, including a five-book series on the history of science and a four-book series on the history of space exploration. As journalists, they covered NASA and related science activities for many years. They have flown on NASA's *Kuiper Airborne Observatory*, covered stories at the Deep Space Network in the Mojave Desert, and experienced zero gravity on experimental NASA flights out of NASA's Ames Research Center. They live in Carmichael, California, with their Boston terrier, F. Scott Fitz).

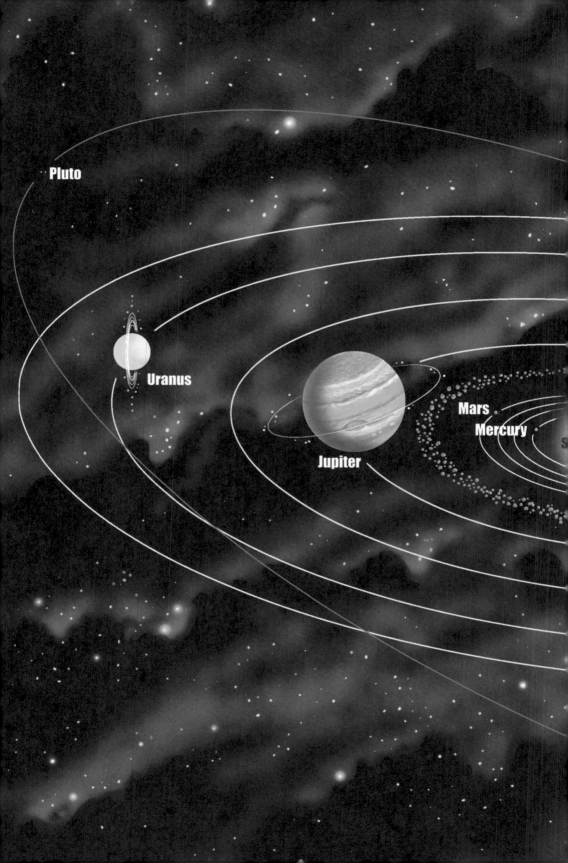

Pluto

Uranus

Jupiter

Mars

Mercury

S